A Tiny Tale Of A Little Brown Dog Called Smudge

By
Kimberly Parr

To order additional copies of this book, contact:
Xlibris
844-714-8691
www.Xlibris.com
Orders@Xlibris.com

ISBN: Softcover   978-1-4257-8826-1

Print information available on the last page

Rev. date: 04/01/2022

Hi,

I am Smudge

This

is a

little

tail

about

me!

I'm way too friendly to be a police dog.

Search Dog;

My nose is Way too short!

Fire Dog?

Way too hot!

Seeing eye dog?

I am Way too short

My master will have to bend over too far to hold onto that fancy handle

Hunting dog?

I could NEVER!

I love All animals

Show dog?

Naaa, too neat and tidy.

I love to play!

Sometimes even in a mud puddle!

Snoozing in the warm sun

knowing my family is close by.

Getting tasty treats.

We all love relaxing at the beach together.

Watching the birds and listening to the water is just so peaceful

I always have lots of fun
when we all play ball together

Now I know what
I was meant to be!

LOVED

by my family

This is the only life for me!

The End

Printed in the United States
by Baker & Taylor Publisher Services